MIRRORS
of
THE SOUL

Kahlil Gibran

MIRRORS
of
THE SOUL

Translated and with
biographical notes by
JOSEPH SHEBAN

CASTLE BOOKS

ISBN 1-55521-896-2

"My soul is my counsel and has taught me to give ear to the voices which are created neither by tongues nor uttered by throats.

"Before my soul became my counsel, I was dull, and weak of hearing, reflecting only upon the tumult and the cry. But, now, I can listen to silence with serenity and can hear in the silence the hymns of ages chanting exaltation to the sky and revealing the secrets of eternity."

KAHLIL GIBRAN

"Mother is everything in this life; she is consolation in time of sorrowing and hope in the time of grieving, and power in the moments of weakness. She is the fountainhead of compassion, forbearance and forgiveness. He who loses his mother loses a bosom upon which he can rest his head, the hand that blesses, and eyes which watch over him."

From *The Broken Wings*

"People are saying that I am the enemy of just laws, of family ties and old tradition. Those people are telling the truth. I do not love man-made laws . . . I love the sacred and spiritual kindness which should be the source of every law upon the earth, for kindness is the shadow of God in man."

From a letter by *Kahlil Gibran* to a cousin

TRANSLATOR'S DEDICATION

To my dear and beloved wife,
Florence, I dedicate this work.

CONTENTS

MIRRORS
of
THE SOUL

1. IS IT ALL POSSIBLE?

Kahlil Gibran, was born in the shadow of the holy Cedars of Lebanon but spent the mature years of his life within the shadows of the skyscrapers of New York. Gibran has been described as The Mystic, The Philosopher, The Religious, The Heretic, The Serene, The Rebellious and The Ageless. Is it possible to accumulate all these contradictory characteristics in one man?

Is it possible for some to burn his books because they are "dangerous, revolutionary and poisonous to youth," while others, at the same moment, are writing: "Gibran, at times, achieves Biblical majesty of phrase. There are echoes of Jesus and echoes of the Old Testament in his words."

One of Gibran's books, *The Prophet,* alone has been on the international best-seller lists for forty years; it has sold more than a million and a half copies and has been translated into more than twenty languages.

The Prophet is Gibran's best work in English, but *The Broken Wings,* his first novel, is considered his

1

best in Arabic. It has been on the international best-seller list longer than *The Prophet*.

Biographers of Gibran, to date, have been his personal friends and acquaintances; they have thus been unable to separate his work from his personal life. They have written only of what they had seen of the Gibran with whom they lived; they were concerned only with the frailties of his life. Biographers, until now, have not tried to explain why the Gibran family migrated to America or to explain the effect of such a migration upon Gibran's work, upon his revolutionary thought or upon his mysticism.

Gibran revolted against law, religion and custom. He advocated a society peaceful and mystical; but the world lacks the procedures and the formulae through which man can discard his present social orders to move into a Utopia full of love and eternal happiness.

Gibran wrote in two languages: Arabic for Lebanon, Syria and the Arabic world; English for the West. His admirers have translated his Arabic works into English, his English works into Arabic. Often, however, the translations have been like transporting an automobile to a country without roads or like training a horse to travel highways and expressways. To understand and justify some of Gibran's writing, a reader must study the unusual environment which influenced the dual Gibran. For example, his biographers have stated that he was exiled from Lebanon, but they have failed to explain that the Lebanese government did not expel Gibran. It was the Turkish Sultan who feared the rebellious Gibran and the introduction of modern

2

Western ideas and Western methods of government into the Arab world which would accelerate the rebellion which was already fermenting against Turkish rule in the Middle East.

2. THE ENVIRONMENT THAT
CREATED GIBRAN

Even before the birth of Gibran, many men had fled from Syria and Lebanon, some settling in Egypt, some in America, others in Europe. Those who were not lucky enough to escape or to be exiled were hanged in the public squares as examples to those who might have been tempted to revolt against the Sultan.

Turkey had conquered Syria as early as the year 1517, over 350 years before Gibran was born (1883). However, the mountains of Lebanon were too treacherous to be assaulted by the Turkish army; hence, Turkey occupied the seashore and the plains and left the mountains and their stubborn inhabitants in control of their own government under the supervision of an agent appointed by Turkey, providing that they paid taxes to the treasury of the Sultans.

The French Revolution

One of the ramifications of the French Revolution in 1790, nearly a century before the birth of Gibran, was the expulsion of the Jesuits from France. Many of these religious were accepted, as refugees, in Lebanon.

The Christians of Lebanon are predominantly Maronites, who are Catholics with extraordinary privileges, which are traditions preserved from the early practices of the Church. The Patriarch, the head of the church in Lebanon, is authorized to appoint bishops, an authority which, of course, is not granted to even Cardinals in the Roman Rite. The Maronite Church uses Syriac, or Aramaic, in its liturgy, the same language spoken by Christ. A Maronite priest may marry. Gibran's mother was the daughter of a Maronite priest, educated in Arabic and French because the Jesuits who had settled permanently in Lebanon had opened schools and taught the French language and Western history, which had not been available in Arabic since the Turks took over three hundred years earlier.

The Sultans, Beautiful Women and Taxes

Turkey was once one of the mightiest nations on earth; it controlled all of the Arab World, North Africa and a great part of Europe. Proud of its military might, Turkey granted its army one-third of the spoils of war. The Sultan, according to law, owned the Empire. In return for good service or for a favor the Sultan was able to bestow an estate upon many of his subjects. This practice recreated and revitalized the feudal system in the Empire. All this favor and practice did not induce the Arab world to become a part of the Turkish Empire; local uprisings and small rebellions continued for many years. In 1860 Youssif Bey Karam, a member on the maternal side of this writer's family and

5

from Gibran's district, led a great revolution for the independence of Lebanon. Although lacking manpower and ammunition, he outmaneuvered and defeated the Turkish Army in several engagements. In the end, however, the revolution failed.

The Sultans, generally speaking, did not help the economy of the Empire; their agents were busy selecting and transporting beautiful girls to the palace. If the girl did not suit the Sultan, she pleased the Wazir or a secondary officer. If she happened to displease her benefactors, her hands were tied, she was placed in a sack and thrown into the sea to drown.

Tax collectors were not regular salaried employees of the government. They would submit bids to the Sultan for the privilege of collecting the tax in a certain country or counties. The tax rate was supposed to be 10 percent of the gross income. However, through intimidation and force those agents collected more than this percentage. If a farmer happened to harvest his wheat before the arrival of the tax collectors, he was accused of having disposed of some of the wheat. If the farmer waited for the tax collector, the wheat was estimated to have a higher yield and collection was made on the higher estimate. Tax collectors often walked into barns, seizing the livestock, and into houses, taking mattresses, cooking utensils and clothing, and selling them for payment of tax. This practice made the Turkish tax rate the highest in the world, without a single benefit accruing to the taxpayer.

The Sultan, as owner of the Empire, had full control of all mineral resources, which remained buried in the ground while the citizens remained in poverty.

6

The Suez Canal

A French engineer, Ferdinand de Lesseps, was in love with a beautiful girl who abandoned him to marry the Emperor Napoleon III. The Empress, to save her former lover from the Emperor's wrath, induced him to leave France.

The wandering lover, de Lesseps, went to Egypt, where he obtained from the Viceroy (who ruled in behalf of the Turkish Sultan) a charter to open a canal from the Mediterranean to the Red Sea. This was not a new idea. Canals had been opened by the Pharaohs, the Arabs, and other rulers of Egypt, but in time they had became useless, being filled by sand drifts from the desert.

After many turbulent years, amid complications and financial difficulties which brought Egypt to the verge of bankruptcy, the Suez Canal was finally ready to be opened. The wandering lover, de Lesseps, anxious to impress his former sweetheart with his magnificent work, induced the Viceroy, Khedive Ismail, to invite the royalty and the dignitaries of Europe to attend the opening of the Canal.

The Khedive, not lacking in gaiety, pomp, or imagination, ordered the building of a new palace to house the guests, and since there was not time to grow trees around the building he ordered grown trees to be moved at a tremendous expense and replanted in the gardens

7

of the new palace. As if this were not enough, he ordered the building of an opera house in which to entertain the guests; this building is the world's oldest opera house still in continuous use.

The Khedive commissioned Verdi, the Italian operatic composer, to set an Egyptian story to Western music. The opera was *Aida*.

What has all this to do with Gibran's life?

In 1869, just fourteen years before Gibran was born, the Empress, Eugénie and her Emperor husband, Napoleon III, boarded the first ship at Port Said and the Canal was formally opened. While the emperors, kings and dignitaries of Europe sat in the opera house listening to the *Aida*, the bugle was sounding the death march for all caravan routes in India, Arabia, Syria, Lebanon, Turkey and even Egypt itself.

The hundreds of thousands of people who raised and sold horses and camels, managed inns and operated caravans, and the merchants who carried on trade between the East and Europe (and all their attendant employees) were out of business. All these routes were within the domain of the Turkish Empire.

It was the straw that broke the camel's back. Until the present day, the Arab world has not recovered from this economically fatal blow. The Sultans of Turkey faced revolutions within their own palaces and brought about their own destruction. Egypt, in bankruptcy, surrendered to the English Army which came to protect English investments in the Canal, received no revenue from the Canal, and its economy never recovered. The Middle East became, theoretically, a sinking ship, its inhabitants abandoning their homes without life preservers.

It was not the poor but the majority of the intellectuals who migrated, the intellectuals who could understand that the economic upheaval was the disastrous result of the canal. Many of them were familiar with the idea of freedom and the Western world through their Jesuit education; many anticipated the permanency of the conditions created by the opening of the canal. Others rebelled against the tax collectors and the tyranny of the Turkish rulers.

Many Syrians and Lebanese migrated into Africa and opened the interior to white European settlers. Many simply boarded ships at Beirut and ended their migration wherever the ship left them, whether it was Australia, South America, New York or Boston.

The Gibran family was among them.

3. THE BIRTHPLACE OF GIBRAN

Man is neither consulted about his birth nor about his death, and he will not be consulted about his eternal abode. Man registers his complaint about his arrival by crying at birth and registers his complaint about leaving this earth by his fear of death.

Gibran registered his birth complaint on the sixth day of December, 1883, at Bcherri in the Republic of Lebanon.

The city of Bcherri perches on a small plateau at the edge of one of the cliffs of Wadi Qadisha. Today there is a paved road to Bcherri, but in Gibran's day there was only a trail which led up the mountain, past the outskirts of the city, then, almost retracing itself, descended to the entrance of the city with its compact homes, built of ivory-hued stones and with rusty, red-tiled roofs.

Before the advent of the helicopter and modern transportation, no army or invader could have entered Bcherri; it was like an unwalled fortress.

Gibran's ancestors millennia ago must have angered the gods, particularly Baal, whose thunder, storm and roaring threw up the ocean bottom and created the chain of mountains from Europe to the Red Sea in Arabia. In the museum at Beirut, there is a rock imbedded with a fish eight or ten million years old. This fish was found in the mountains, not far from Bcherri.

10

This work of the gods left deep canyons and cliffs, the deepest of which is Wadi Qadisha, meaning holy or sacred valley. It begins by the seashore and it ends near the summit, traveling along this great valley. Gibran as well as modern tourists could not but ponder the force that raised the strata of rocks on its side thrusting toward the sky, and created out of the ocean floor a wave-like ribbon of mountains stretching out for miles.

Barbara Young, a friend and biographer of Gibran, wrote: "To visit the Wadi Qadisha is to leave the modern world and to be plunged body and spirit into an atmosphere both ancient and timeless.

"It is a beauty of a wild and unbridled quality, and it has a mighty force that compels the mind to dwell upon the words we have for eternity."

These mountains of Lebanon for centuries were covered with cedars, mentioned in the Bible more than 103 times. They are called the "cedars of God" and "the Cedar in the paradise of God." Now the cedar forest near Gibran's home is called the holy cedar. If the guardianship of this forest were awarded to the nearest large city, Bcherri would be entitled to the honor. Gibran's grandfather being a priest, the family would have had the first claim to the keys of the "Cedars of God." Gibran's ancestors, the Phoenicians, celebrated their religious rites among these cedars.

The oldest recorded stories, like those of Gelgamish, Eshtar and Tamuz, took place in the forest of the cedar.[1] Gibran walked, slept and meditated in the

1. See the chapters on Gelgamish, Eshtar and Tamuz in the author's book *One White Race*.

shadow of the cedars. He read about the ancient gods and the history of the cedar and how it was used in the palaces of the ancient empires of Assyria, Babylonia and in the temples of Jerusalem and in the coffins of the Pharaohs. It was cedar wood that gave the Phoenician ships extra strength, resilience and resistance to the elements.

Gibran, living in the shadows of the skyscrapers of New York, never forgot the cedars in the paradise of God, and never forgot the gods who lived and played in that paradise. It was reflected in the mirror of his soul; it was reflected in his work. In a letter to his cousin Gibran wrote: "The things which the child loves remain in the domain of the heart until old age. The most beautiful thing in life is that our souls remain hovering over the places where we once enjoyed ourselves. I am one of those who remembers those places regardless of distance or time."

In his book *Jesus the Son of Man* in the chapter "The Woman from Byblos" Gibran wrote:

"Weep with me, ye daughters of Ashtarte, and all ye
    lovers of Tamouz.
Bid your heart melt and rise and run blood-tears,
For He who was made of gold and ivory is no more.
In the dark forest the boar overcame Him,
And the tusks of the boar pierced His flesh.
Now He lies stained with the leaves of yesteryear,
And no longer shall His footsteps wake the seeds
    that sleep in the bosom of Spring.
His voice will not come with the dawn to my window,
And I shall be forever alone.

Weep with me, ye daughters of Ashtarte, and all ye
    lovers of Tamouz,
For my Beloved has escaped me;
He who spoke as the rivers speak;
He whose voice and time were twins;
He whose mouth was a red pain made sweet;
He on whose lips gall would turn to honey.

Weep with me, daughters of Ashtarte, and ye lovers
    of Tamouz.
Weep with me around His bier as the stars weep,
And as the moon-petals fall upon His wounded body.
Wet with your tears the silken covers of my bed,
Where my Beloved once lay in my dream,
And was gone away in my awakening.

I charge ye, daughters of Ashtarte, and all ye lovers
    of Tamouz,
Bare your breasts and weep and comfort me,
For Jesus of Nazareth is dead."

Byblos was not one of the mightiest Phoenician cities,
but it was the greatest religious center. The Old Testament was called the Book of Byblos. The head deity of
that city was El, the father of all gods. El is the name
in the Bible often called Elohim, and in Arabic is called
Elah. The earliest alphabetical writing was discovered
in Byblos. Gibran, attending school in Beirut, must
have passed through Byblos and Tripoli each time he
went home on visits. Byblos is on the seashore, north
of Beirut, and a full day's journey on horseback from
Bcherri.

Gibran's knowledge of geography and history was not limited to his home town or the school route. His description of places, events, customs and history of the Middle East prove that he had visited those places. Gibran was twelve years of age when he came to the United States. After two years of schooling in Boston he was back in Lebanon finishing his education. During the summer his father took him all over Lebanon, Syria and Palestine. After four years of studying Arabic and French, he left for Greece, Rome, Spain and then Paris to do more studying. After two years of study in Paris, Gibran returned to Boston.

Among the places Gibran visited were Nazareth, Bethlehem, Jerusalem, Tyre (Sidon), Tripoli, Baalbek, Damascus, Aleppo and Palmyra. These names are but small dots on the map of the world, but they must have had profound effect on the thinking, the writings and philosophy of Gibran. They are reflected in the mirrors of his soul and in every word he wrote. It is reasonable to assume that while Gibran's feet were stumbling on the stones of Nazareth, he decided to write his book *Jesus the Son of Man*.

Baalbek is one of the wonders of the world; among its strewn stones and columns a man stands in humility, bowing his head to the skill, might and devotion of its builders to their gods. Baalbek was built east of one of the highest summits of the chain of mountains confining the Mediterranean; the cedar forest is on the west side of this summit, and Gibran's humble home was a short distance from both of them.

Baalbek was the oldest and the greatest religious

center of the white man; the Egyptian Pharaohs placed boats of cedar wood near their tombs to transport them, on the day of resurrection, across the Mediterranean into Baalbek. The god Baal was found in all of the holy places of the white man, from Babylonia to the Baltic Sea.[2] The greatest competition to Jehovah came from Baal and his mother, Eshtar. Baal created the rain for everything living; but he was also temperamental and in his anger created storms, lightning and earthquakes. How could Gibran remove him from the mirrors of his soul when he gazed daily at Wadi Qadisha, created by the anger of this god? Who is to say that Gibran's book *The Earth's Gods* was not conceived on the cliffs of Bcherri, or amid the ruins of Baalbek? Within this book, Baalbek was the setting for many articles dealing with religion and mystic life.

Damascus, the oldest continuously inhabited city in the world, was the capital of the golden period of Islam. While Europe was in its dark ages, its rulers unable to sign their own names, and while numbers and science were considered the work of the devil, the Ommiad dynasty at Damascus was gathering learned men from the four corners of the empire, which stretched from Spain to India, an area greater than any empire preceding it. These men translated the works of the Persians, the Greeks and the Romans and added their own. The outcome of this labor was preserved and translated into the modern languages after the Crusades. In other words, the works of the Greeks were translated into Arabic and from Arabic into English.

2. See chapter on Baal in the book, *One White Race.*

15

Wandering in the streets and mosques of Damascus, Gibran realized the absence of pictures of the great Arab leaders. This was due to the fact that Islam prohibits the use of images. Before he reached the age of sixteen, Gibran studied the works of the Arab philosophers and poets, and to match the written characters, he etched a set of pictures depicting those men and women.

Among the cities near the birthplace of Gibran were Tyre and Sidon. They were the main Phoenician cities which carried trade and civilization to the known world; they colonized and civilized Greece; they founded the city of Rome; they colonized North Africa and developed constitutional government in Carthage (this system originated in Tripoli, which is on the road between Bcherri and Beirut). It was carried thence into Carthage, and from that great Phoenician city was copied in America and became the great document known as the United States Constitution, under which Gibran lived to write in freedom for both Arabic and English readers. This small piece of land, the birthplace of Gibran, was the birthplace of Western Civilization and constitutional government, and Gibran was one of its blessed sons and the latest contribution to this great United States of America.

4. WORDS OF CAUTION

Lebanon or Syria?

Gibran is known as the man from Lebanon, but he wrote *My Country Syria*. This discrepancy creates a most vexing problem for anyone writing about the Middle East.

As guideposts we offer the following:

As rivers bring sediment into the sea, new areas of land are created and new cities follow the land; in that case one city is older than another. In the Middle East the bottom of the ocean rose, carrying its petrified fish to the summit of a mountain. All the land east of the Mediterranean was created at the same time; no one section of it is older than another.

Man roamed the land as a hunter in the Middle East and North Africa for hundreds of thousands, if not millions of years. During this period of hunting there were no political subdivisions and man needed no passport to migrate.[1] Europe was covered with snow until twenty-five thousand years ago. Hence it was not conducive to human habitation; a few handy savages lived in caves until the glacier receded. Then man changed his residence from a cave to a sur, or enclosure, and became a city dweller; this sur became

1. See the book *One White Race*.

17

the name of a city on the seashore known to the West as Tyre. This city, Sur (Tyre), and its goddess Suria, which is still worshiped in India, gave its name to the whole area east of the Mediterranean. As Sur was latinized into Tyre, Suria was latinized into Syria and included the mountains of Lebanon.

Those city dwellers developed a philosophy of the existence of the soul, its immortality and resurrection, along with the premise that the soul needed help or guidance in order that it might reach paradise (heaven). This idea was adopted by St. Augustine. Those city dwellers of Sur or Tyre, traveled with their philosophy to Egypt, Babylonia, North Africa and Europe; they conquered the seas, colonized and founded the great cities of Europe, including London. They were nick-named the Phoenicians or "the believers in immor-tality."

In the caves men developed the idea of fighting in groups to overcome the mighty animals; in the city they fought in groups to destroy each other.

The cave dwellers grouped together to protect a cave or a spring of water; the Suri or city dwellers built a sur to protect a city and an army to protect a country. Even now every country keeps an army.

What has all this to do with the nationality of Gibran?

It affects us in this respect: wars create new bound-aries, new administrations and new philosophies of government. Hence the administrative divisions of Gibran's country during the Roman period varied greatly at different times. The Roman Emperor, Hadrian, divided it into three provinces: Syria, Syria-Phoenicia and Syria-Palestine. Gibran was born in Syria-Phoenicia; Christ was born in Syria-Palestine.

One historian writing about the birth of Christ has said: "It did not appear that one born in the obscurity of a Syrian provincial village would be able to give a new date to history and change the religious belief of mankind."

After the Romans came the Arabs, after the Arabs came the Turks, after the Turks came the French and the English. None of the armies of these invaders ever assaulted the mountains because they were treacherous, impregnable and not worth the cost. These mountains were like a besieged city; the armies would occupy the plains on the east and the cities along the seashore, and after a period of time the mountaineers would come down to join each new invader, bargaining but reserving for themselves certain rights and privileges.

When the Arabs conquered that part of the world from India to Spain and converted it to Islam, the mountaineers, Gibran's ancestors, were able to preserve their Christian religion, a tiny island of Christians in an ocean of Islam.

When Turkey overran the country, it divided Syria into districts (*Wilayah*), naming for each one a governor with the title of Pasha. The people during the Turkish rule of four hundred years, refused to be assimilated by their conquerors. Hence the country of Gibran remained its Achilles' heel, and its numerous revolutions were supported by one European country or another until 1860, when a civil war broke out.

England sent her fleet and France disembarked on Lebanese soil an army of six thousand men. After the landing of these armies, a special committee composed of diplomatic representatives of Franc., England, Russia and Austria convened in Beirut with the First Minister of Turkey. The outcome was the conferring upon Lebanon of an internal autonomy guaranteed by these European powers. The Sultan was to appoint a Christian governor for Lebanon and the European powers were to approve the appointment. This autonomous area included neither the plains of Bekaa on the east nor the cities along the seashores, nor even Beirut, which is now the capital of Lebanon.

Therefore, the people who came to America from the eastern shores of the Mediterranean were classified as Syrian nationals regardless of whether they came from Damascus or from the mountains by the cedars.

After the First World War Turkey was ousted and France received from the League of Nations a mandate over Syria and Lebanon, while England took over Palestine. Even then, people arriving in America were listed as Syrian nationals.

During the Second World War, Lebanon and Syria overthrew the French mandate and became separate, independent countries with full representation in the United Nations.

Therefore the words in Gibran's book *My Countrymen the Syrians* include both the Syrians and the Lebanese.

"During the days of my youth I wrote enough prose and poetry to fill many volumes, but I did not, and shall not, commit the crime of having them published."

Thus wrote Gibran to a friend. However, the admirers of Gibran are publishing anything and everything they can find. As a matter of fact, his best friend did the same thing while Gibran was still alive. Gibran protested, "Don't mention to me my past deeds, for the remembrance of them makes my blood into a burning fire."

This does not mean that all the early works of Gibran were trivial or unimportant, especially when we consider that Gibran died at the age of forty-eight (December 6, 1883 — April 10, 1931).

A word of caution: Keep in mind that many items now in book form were originally written in a letter to a friend or in an article to a newspaper.

Reprints

Most, if not all, of Gibran's works have been through numerous reprints. Some of these reprints fail to carry the date of the original publication or the date and source of the material, particularly the Arabic editions, whose front page carries the year of reprint.

How can future biographers determine the time and circumstances under which a newspaper article was written?

For example, the Arabic edition reads: *"Spirits*

Rebellious by Gibran, 1959." The English edition, published by Heinemann, reads: "The Spirits Rebellious by Gibran, translated from Arabic; first published 1949." But the introduction explains that the stories were completed in 1908.

Barbara Young wrote that the book was written and burned in the market place in Beirut between 1901 and 1903.

Quotation Marks

There are no quotation marks in Arabic writing. However, Arabic students of English or French do use quotation marks, often haphazardly.

One Lebanese biographer wrote some paragraphs in Arabic, using quotation marks, describing them as the work of Gibran. In reality, the quotation marks were meant to signify that they were figments of the biographer's own imagination. In translation these marks were not removed. A biographer writing in English, especially one who is not familiar with the Arabic language, accepts the quotation marks as an indication that the statements are Gibran's own saying and beliefs.

This confusion is unfair to Gibran, unfair to future writers and unfair to the reader. Therefore these words of caution become imperative.

5. GIBRAN'S DUAL PERSONALITY

Man is the product of his environment. When Gibran was born, the economic conditions of the Middle East were bad and political conditions were even worse. For many years Turkey had been involved in wars, of which she was always the loser. Thus, the boundaries of the Empire were shrinking. Meanwhile, inside Turkey, the government grew more and more tyrannical. Minority groups in all parts of the Empire were abused and persecuted. It was true that the Lebanese were exempt from military service because of the local autonomy granted them in 1860 under pressure of the European nations, but it was also true that many families were moving from the cities into the mountains to avoid the dreaded military service. Many Moslem families changed to Christianity.

The whole Arab world became honeycombed with secret societies working to throw off the Turkish yoke. The Turkish government, trusting no one, systematically discharged non-Turks from government offices and replaced them with Turkish citizens; even judges were removed from their high offices. These secret societies even dared to send delegates to an Arab conference held in Paris. Many Syrian and Lebanese men from America attended the conference and made demands for reform. Many of the leaders paid with their lives.

They were hanged in public squares for others to see and take heed.

Gibran, a young man in the United States and beyond the rope of the hangman, called his countrymen to revolt. He wrote articles for Arabic publication, using the words, "my countrymen." These articles translated into English without benefit of explanations gave the impression that Gibran was calling the people of his adopted country of America to rebellion. Hence we find in Gibran a dual personality; he wrote in Arabic calling for arms, and in English calling for contentment and peace.

The following is an example of Gibran's writing to his countrymen, published in translation without explanation:

My Countrymen

by Kahlil Gibran

What do you seek of me my countrymen?
Do you wish that I falsely promise to build
For you great palaces out of words, and temples
    roofed with dreams?
Or would you rather I destroy the work of liars
    and cowards and demolish the work of
    hypocrites and tyrants?
What would you have me do, My Countrymen?

Shall I coo like a pigeon to please you,
Or shall I roar like a lion to please myself?
I sang for you but you did not dance;

I lamented but you did not cry.
Do you wish that I sing and lament at the same time?
Your souls are hungry and the bread of knowledge
    is more plentiful than the stones of the valleys,
    but you do not eat.
Your hearts thirst, yet the springs of life pour around
    your homes like rivers, and you do not drink.
The sea has its ebb and tide, the moon its crescent
    and fullness, and the year has its seasons of
    summer and winter, but Justice never changes,
    never falters, never perishes.
Why, then, do you attempt to distort the truth?

I have called you in the quietness of the night
    to point out to you the beauty of the moon and
    the dignity of the stars. You arise, frightened,
    and unsheathing your swords, cry, "Where is the
    enemy — to be struck down?"
At dawn, when the horsemen of the enemy arrived,
    I called again, but you refused to rise. You
    remained asleep, at war with the enemy in your
    dreams.

I told you, "Let us climb to the summit of the
    mountain where I can show you the kingdoms of
    the world." You answered saying, "In the bottom
    of the valley of this mountain our fathers and
    forefathers lived; and in its shadows they died;
    and in its caves were they buried. How shall we
    leave and go to places to which they did not go?"
I told you, "Let us go to the plains and I will

25

show you gold mines and treasures of the earth."
You refused, saying, "In the plains lurk thieves
and robbers."

I told you, "Let us go to the seashore where the
sea gives of its bounties." You refused, saying,
"The tumult of the abyss frightens us to death."

I loved you, My Countrymen, yet my love for
you distressed me and did not benefit you.
Today I hate you, and hate is a flood that carries
away the dead branches and washes away
crumbling buildings.
I pitied your weakness, but my pity encouraged
your sloth. . . .

What are your demands from me, My Countrymen?
Rather what are your demands from Life,
Although no longer do I consider you children
of Life.
Your souls cringe in the palms of soothsayers
and sorcerers, while your bodies tremble in the
paws of the bloody tyrants, and your country
lies prostrate under the heels of the conquerors:
what do you expect as you stand before the face
of the sun? Your swords are rusty; the points
of your spears are broken; your shields are
covered with mud. Why, then, do you stand
upon the battlefield?
Hypocrisy is your religion; Pretension, your
life; dust, your end.
Why do you live? Death is the only rest for
the wretched.

Life is determination in youth, strife during
        manhood, and wisdom in maturity. But you,
        My Countrymen, were born old and feeble,
        your heads shrunk,
Your skin withered, and you became as children,
        playing in the mire, and throwing stones at
        one another. . . .

Humanity is a crystalline river, singing, in a
        rippling rush, and carrying the secrets of the
        mountains to the depths of the sea. But you
        are as a swamp with worms in its dregs and
        snakes on its banks.

The soul is a sacred, blue-burning flame,
        illuminating the faces of the gods. But your
        souls, My Countrymen, are ashes for the wind to
        scatter over the snows, and for the tempest to
        dispel into the deep abysses.

I hate you, My Countrymen, because you despise
        glory and greatness.

I vilify you because you vilify yourselves.

I am your enemy because you are enemies of the
        gods and you do not know it.

The day of reckoning came during the First World
War. Turkey entered the war on the side of Germany
and the troops of both countries occupied the shores
east of the Mediterranean. This action was to prevent

27

a landing by the Allies and, more important, it was to protect the railroad line that carried food to Turkey and Germany, preventing a complete blockade of Germany.

Lebanon, demanding autonomy, had finally been given that privilege. To start with, Lebanon was not self-sufficient. Now that it was being blockaded, it was deprived of the importation of food. Then the locusts came, for two solid years, to eat everything from the smallest blade of grass to the old oaks. The inhabitants died of starvation on the roads and sidewalks and inside their houses. The leaders were picked up and hanged in the public squares; if the war had lasted longer the extermination would have been complete and no one would have been left to tell the story.

Gibran, reacting to this tragedy, wrote in Arabic the article, "My People Died," part of which follows:

My People Died

by Gibran

My people died of starvation and I came here alive, lamenting them in my loneliness. . . .

I am told, 'The tragedy of your country is only a part of the tragedy of the world; the tears and the blood shed in your country are only drops in the river of blood and tears pouring night and day in the valleys and the plains of the world.'

This may be true, but the tragedy of my people is a silent one conceived in the heads of men, whom we should call snakes and serpents. The tragedy of my people is without music and without parades.

If my people had revolted against the tyrants and died in defiance, I would have said that death for liberty was more honorable than the life of servitude.

Whoever reaches eternity with sword in his hand lives as long as there is justice.

If my countrymen had entered the World War and were destroyed in battle to the last man, I would have said it was a wild hurricane destroying the green and the dead branches; I would have said death under the force of a hurricane is better than life in the arms of old age.

If an earthquake had swallowed my people and loved ones, I would have said it is the law of Nature directed by a power beyond the comprehension of man. It is foolish to attempt to solve its mysteries.

But my people did not die in rebellion, did not die in a battle and they were not buried by an earthquake.

My people died on the cross. My people died with their arms stretched toward both East and West and their eyes seeking in the darkness of the skies.

They died in silence because the ears of humanity had become deaf to their cry.

They died but they were not criminals.

They died because they were peaceful.

They died in the land that produced milk and honey.

They died because the hellish serpent seized all their flocks and all the harvest of their fields.

After the war France took over Syria and Lebanon, through a mandate from the League of Nations, to help them organize governments and become independent within three years.

The three years dragged into six, into twelve, and it appeared as though the French were to stay in Lebanon forever.

Gibran, in reaction to this situation, wrote his article, "You Have Your Lebanon and I Have My Lebanon."

"You Have Your Lebanon and I Have My Lebanon"

by Gibran

You have your Lebanon and its dilemma. I have my Lebanon and its beauty.

Your Lebanon is an arena for men from the West and men from the East.

My Lebanon is a flock of birds fluttering in the early morning as shepherds lead their sheep into the meadow and rising in the evening as farmers return from their fields and vineyards.

You have your Lebanon and its people. I have my Lebanon and its people.

Yours are those whose souls were born in the hospitals of the West; they are as a ship without rudder or sail upon a raging sea. . . . They are strong and eloquent among themselves but weak and dumb among Europeans.

They are brave, the liberators and the reformers, but only in their own area. But they are the cowards, always led backward by the Europeans. They are those who croak like frogs boasting that they have rid themselves of their ancient, tyrannical enemy, but the truth of the matter is that this tyrannical enemy still hides within their own souls. They are the slaves for whom time had exchanged rusty chains for shiny ones so that they thought themselves free. These are the children of your Lebanon. Is there anyone among them who represents the strength of the towering rocks of Lebanon, the purity of its water or the fragrance of its air? Who among them vouchsafes to say, "When I die I leave my country little better than when I was born?"

Who among them dares to say, "My life was a drop of blood in the veins of Lebanon, a tear in her eyes or a smile upon her lips?"

Those are the children of your Lebanon. They are,

in your estimation, great; but insignificant in my estimation.

Let me tell you who are the children of my Lebanon.

They are the farmers who would turn fallow field
into garden and grove.

They are the shepherds who lead their flocks through
the valleys to be fattened for your table meat and your
woolens.

They are the vine-pressers who press the grape to
wine and boil it to syrup.

They are the parents who tend the nurseries, the
mothers who spin silken yarn.

They are the husbands who harvest the wheat and
the wives who gather the sheaves.

They are the builders, the potters, the weavers and
the bell-casters.

They are the poets who pour their souls in new cups.

They are those who migrate with nothing but courage
in their hearts and strength in their arms but who return with wealth in their hands and a wreath of glory
upon their heads.

They are the victorious wherever they go and loved
and respected wherever they settle.

They are the ones born in huts but who died in
palaces of learning.

These are the children of Lebanon; they are the
lamps that cannot be snuffed by the wind and the salt
which remains unspoiled through the ages.

They are the ones who are steadily moving toward
perfection, beauty and truth.

What will remain of your Lebanon after a century?

Tell me! Except bragging, lying and stupidity? Do you expect the ages to keep in its memory the traces of deceit and cheating and hypocrisy? Do you think the atmosphere will preserve in its pockets the shadows of death and the stench of graves?

Do you believe life will accept a patched garment for a dress? Verily, I say to you that an olive plant in the hills of Lebanon will outlast all of your deeds and your works; that the wooden plow pulled by the oxen in the crannies of Lebanon are nobler than your dreams and aspirations.

I say to you, while the conscience of time listened to me, that the songs of a maiden collecting herbs in the valleys of Lebanon will outlast all the uttering of the most exalted prattler among you. I say to you that you are achieving nothing. If you knew that you are accomplishing nothing, I would feel sorry for you, but you know it not.

You have Your Lebanon and I have My Lebanon.

[As Gibran bitterly assailed the politicians in Lebanon he tenderly expressed his hopes and belief in the young people of Lebanese and Syrian origin in America. The following message is often found, framed and displayed on the walls in the homes of Gibran's countrymen:]*

---

*Sections in brackets are editor's interpolations within Gibran's text.

I Believe in You

by Gibran

I believe in you, and I believe in your destiny.

I believe that you are contributors to this new civilization.

I believe that you have inherited from your fore-fathers an ancient dream, a song, a prophecy, which you can proudly lay as a gift of gratitude upon the lap of America.

I believe that you can say to the founders of this great nation, "Here I am, a youth, a young tree whose roots were plucked from the hills of Lebanon, yet I am deeply rooted here, and I would be fruitful."

And I believe that you can say to Abraham Lincoln, the blessed, "Jesus of Nazareth touched your lips when you spoke, and guided your hand when you wrote; and I shall uphold all that you have said and all that you have written."

I believe that you can say to Emerson and Whitman and James, "In my veins runs the blood of the poets and wise men of old, and it is my desire to come to you and receive, but I shall not come with empty hands."

I believe that even as your fathers came to this land to produce riches, you were born here to produce riches by intelligence, by labor.

I believe that it is in you to be good citizens.

And what is it to be a good citizen?

It is to acknowledge the other person's rights before

asserting your own, but always to be conscious of your own.

It is to be free in word and deed, but it is also to know that your freedom is subject to the other person's freedom.

It is to create the useful and the beautiful with your own hands, and to admire what others have created in love and with faith.

It is to produce by labor and only by labor, and to spend less than you have produced that your children may not be dependent upon the state for support when you are no more.

It is to stand before the towers of New York and Washington, Chicago and San Francisco saying in your heart, "I am the descendant of a people that builded Damascus and Byblos, and Tyre and Sidon and Antioch, and now I am here to build with you, and with a will."

You should be proud of being an American, but you should also be proud that your fathers and mothers came from a land upon which God laid His gracious hand and raised His messengers.

Young Americans of Syrian origin, I believe in you.

[Gibran did not live long enough to enjoy the realization of his hopes and dreams. The Lebanon of Gibran succeeded finally in becoming an independent nation.

In the summer of 1964, the Lebanese Government dedicated a four-lane boulevard stretching from Beirut to the gracious International Airport, the name of the avenue being Jadat Al Mogtaribeen (Lebanese Overseas). This boulevard is the path Gibran walked to meet his first love, and it encompasses the dreams toward which Gibran prodded his beloved homeland: the graceful resorts, modern skyscrapers and luxurious hotels of Beirut and the jet-age accommodations at the airfield. Each day, the emigrants born here in poverty travel Gibran's path. "The young trees, rooted in the hills of Lebanon, transplanted to various parts of the world, return, and they are fruitful."

In my mind's eye, I see Gibran watching this new, passing parade. For did he not write:

"A little while, a moment to rest upon the wind, and another woman shall bear me."]

6. GIBRAN'S PAINTING AND POETRY

The religion of Islam prohibited the use of images and idols, even the image of Mohammed. In the Christian countries it conquered, Islam converted many of the churches into mosques. Statues and paintings were easily removed; mosaic walls were covered with plaster. Hence the art of painting and carving vanished from the Islamic world. To enhance the appearance of new buildings, architects and decorators resorted to lines, geometrical designs and scenery.

As a young student in Lebanon, Gibran was not influenced by the art of one particular man or school of painters. Studying the work of the Arab philosophers, Gibran imagined their appearances and for the first time etched likenesses of these men appeared in books. Gibran created these at the age of seventeen. In the early days of his career as a painter, he exhibited his work in a studio in Boston. A fire destroyed the building and the entire collection of drawings and paintings. This was a great shock to a young man who needed to sell his work for a living. In later years he remarked that it was just as well that they were destroyed because he was not fully mature when he painted them. The paintings and drawings of Gibran are now scattered all over the Middle East, Europe and America.

Early in his career, Gibran wrote books, poetry and articles in Arabic. He created a new era in style, influenced by Western thought, and a revolution in the minds of the younger generation of his country. But all this did not give him a living income; therefore in his art he concentrated on portraits of famous or rich people. The illustrations for his books consisted basically of naked bodies, shadows drawn in gray and black. Their movements and the settings were a clear attempt to relate the known to the unknown, to depict love, sorrow, and life in their relation to man and God. He used no clothes, no trees, no buildings, no churches, and nothing to identify the scene with any section of the earth or any religious denomination. What is revealed is Gibran and his own connection with the handiwork of God. Gibran's ancestors conceived of God as an ancient father with long beard and flowing clothes; this conception remained with the church which supported and financed the work of the great men of the Middle Ages. Gibran, not supported by the church, not affected by any specific style in his childhood, remained free to develop his own style.

Gibran left few poems because he learned how to write Arabic poetry before he knew how to write English. This has been the case of other Arabic writers in Gibran's circumstances. According to the rules of Arabic poetry, what we call a poem in English is considered only a rhymed phrase. In other words, if we accept the Arabic rules as standard, the English language has no poetry.

Gibran wrote most of his Arabic poetry in the early years of his life. Arab poets prided themselves in using words that could be understood only after consulting the dictionary. Gibran's Arabic poetry opened a new era and new horizons by using short and simple words.

In his later years, Gibran wrote for English readers. As we have said, according to Gibran's education, writing poetry in English would be like taking the work of Shakespeare and rewriting it in ordinary language. Hence, we find very little poetry among the voluminous work of Gibran.

In what poetry he wrote, the philosophy was the same as in his prose. The following translation gives an example of this philosophy:

"During the ebb, I wrote a line upon the sand,
Committing to it all that is in my soul and mind;
I returned at the tide to read it and to ponder upon it,
I found naught upon the seashore but my ignorance."

One of Gibran's Arabic poems, The Procession, has been translated into English by two different writers. Comparing the two works we find great variation and we feel that something is missing. If I were to attempt a translation, I could probably do no better. There remains something inherently untranslatable in the basic use of words and language. One of the translators wrote: "By reason of the nebulous, untranslatable character of the Arabic language . . . it required occasional departure from strict translation in order that Gibran's mighty message be captured intact."

A commentator who knew Arabic has said: "Arabic is a forceful language with a prolific vocabulary of pregnant words of fine shadings. Its delicate tones of warmth and color form with its melodies a symphony, the sound of which moves its listeners to tears or ecstasy."

Though we lose some of the forcefulness and melody, even a translation conveys the basic philosophy of Gibran, which reached its peak of expression in the later work, *The Prophet*.

The translator, G. Kheirallah, said of this work: "The poem represents the unconscious autobiography of Gibran: Gibran the sage, mellowed beyond his years, and Gibran the rebel, who had come to believe in the Unity and Universality of all existence and who longed for simple, impersonal freedom, merged in harmony with all things."

7. THE PHILOSOPHY OF GIBRAN

"A philosopher is an ordinary person who thinks more deeply and obstinately than other people."

The American philosopher, William James, defines philosophy as "an unusually stubborn attempt to think clearly."

The word "Philosophy" comes from Greek and means "love of wisdom." It is the process of observing the facts and events of life, in both the mental and the physical worlds, with intelligent analysis of their causes and effects, and especially the laws that govern them, for the purpose of deducing sets of general principles and concepts, usually with some practical application of these as a final goal.

Because we live in such a complex and distracting world, few of us see the effect of the principles of the great philosophers upon our lives, our relations with each other and indeed upon the very concepts we take for granted. For example, even hunger is a much more sophisticated process to man today than in the past: he measures his desire for food not merely by his appetite and the accessibility of foodstuffs, but also by his ability to pay for it and his peculiar tastes. This self-control is the result, of course, of thousands of years of legal, religious and political training.

41

Our world is so complex that we take for granted engineering processes that would dwarf any of the ancient Seven Wonders of the World; we ride railroad tracks that do not follow faithfully the curvature of the earth, for the train would jump the tracks if they were level. We pass skyscrapers whose stress and strain are figured to the millionth of an inch, yet take for granted the fact that the Empire State Building actually sways constantly many feet. If we are religiously inclined, we take going to the church of our choice for granted; if we are non-believers, we give no second thought to the fact that we do not have to attend religious services if we do not choose. Yet the very privilege of non-belief represents the victory of philosophy; otherwise the non-churchgoer would still face the lions or the stake.

Gibran did not write treatises about philosophy; but as soon as he began his great book *The Prophet,* dealing with the question of birth and death, he placed himself within the Socratic maxim: "Know thyself."

A woman hailed him, asking, "Prophet of God . . . tell us all that has been shown you of that which is between birth and death."

As soon as Gibran wrote, "I did not love man-made laws and I abhor the traditions that our ancestors left us," he placed himself in the sphere of the theologians, illustrating particularly one of the principles of St. Augustine: "One could not doubt unless he were alive and thinking and aware that there is such a thing as truth."

Before man was able to read or write he pondered

the meaning of his existence on earth. He came from where? He was going where? And why?

And as man learned to write, though in a simple and crude manner, he left for us his conception of life and death. Modern writers called this writing philosophy.

However, in these few pages, we cannot explore at length this great and vast subject, examples of which fill the shelves of libraries throughout the world. We will attempt to determine only the belief and reflections in the heart and soul of Gibran. Much of his writing reveals that he asked himself the same perplexing questions as ancient man. He did accept the premise that there is a God, but was criticized for his definition of God.

Gibran's ancestors in Lebanon and the Middle East described God as a merciful Father and hewed His image from rock in the likeness of an old man with a long beard. This conception was expressed in the three great religions of the West: Judaism, Christianity and Islam.

Some philosophers, particularly the Arabic ones, searched for a more comprehensive definition of God.

Averröes (1126-1198), a great Arabic philosopher, wrote that a simple-minded believer would say, "God is in heaven." However, he said, "A man of trained mind, knowing that God must not be represented as a physical entity in space, would say, 'God is everywhere, and not merely in Heaven.'

"But if the omnipresence of God be taken only in a physical and special sense, that formula, too, is likely in error.

"Accordingly, the philosopher more adequately expresses the purely spiritual nature of God when he asserts that God is nowhere but in Himself; in fact, rather than say that God is in space he might more justly say that space and matter are in God."

Gibran, educated in Lebanon, must have accepted the explanation of Averröes. In his *Garden of the Prophet,* he has one in a group of men ask, "Master, we hear much talk of God hereabout. What say you of God, and Who is He in very truth?" Gibran answered saying: "Think now, My Beloved, of a heart that contains all your hearts, a love that ecompasses all your loves, a spirit that encompasses all your spirits, a voice enfolding all your voices, and a silence deeper than all your silences, and timeless.

"Seek now to perceive in your self-fullness a beauty more enchanting than all things beautiful, a song more vast than the songs of the seas and the forest, a majesty. . . .

"It were wiser to speak less of God, Whom we cannot understand, and more of each other, whom we may understand. Yet I would have you know that we are the breath and the fragrance of God. We are God, in leaf, in flower, and oftentimes in fruit."

When it came to questions about the soul the biographers and critics of Gibran were at a loss. Some biographers said that Gibran believed in the transmigration of the soul, which is better known as the doctrine of Nirvana. Others, because Gibran assailed the activities of some religious men, accused him of being a heretic.

Therefore, to understand the philosophy of Gibran, we must discard part of what his biographers have written and consider objectively what Gibran himself wrote. He wrote many articles in Arabic about the great philosophers, among them Avicenna, Al Farid and Al Ghazali. Gibran regarded the belief of Avicenna nearest to his own. The following are Gibran's words translated from the Arabic:

"A Compendium on the Soul" by Avicenna

by Gibran

There is no poem written by the ancient poets nearer my own beliefs and my spiritual inclination than that poem of Avicenna, "A Compendium on the Soul."

In this sublime poem, the old sage embodies the greatest hopes engendered by man's aspiration and knowledge, the deepest well of imagination created by man's thinking; and he raises those questions which are the first in man's quest and those theories which result from great thought and long meditation.

It is not strange for such a poem to come from the awareness of Avicenna, the genius of his age; but it is paradoxical for it to be the manifestation of the man who spent his life probing into the secrets of the body, into the peculiarities of physical matter. I believe he reached the mystery of the soul by studying physical matter, thus comprehending the unknown through the known. His poem, therefore, provides clear proof that knowledge is the life of the mind, and that practical experiments lead to intellectual conclusions, to spiritual feelings and to God.

The reader is bound to find, among the great writers of the West, passages which remind him of this sublime

46

poem. For example, there are lines in Shakespeare's immortal plays similar to this one of Avicenna:

"I despised my arrival on this earth and I despise my departure; it is a tragedy."

There is a resemblance to the writing of Shelley in the following:

"I dozed, and in a revelation, I saw what it is not possible to see with open eyes."

There is in the writing of Browning this parallel thought: "It shone like lightning, but it vanished as if it had never shone."

Nonetheless, the sage preceded all these English writers by centuries, yet he embodied in a single poem ideas which have appeared in a variety of writers of many ages. This is what confirms Avicenna as the genius not only of his century but of the centuries following and makes his poem "A Compendium on the Soul" the most sublime poem ever composed upon this most glorious subject.[1]

Al Farid

Al Farid was a devout poet. His unquenchable soul drank the divine wine of the spirit, wandering intoxicated through the exotic world where dwell the dreams of poets, lovers and mystics. Then, sobered, his soul

1. In the field of medicine, the books of Avicenna remained basic textbooks of the universities of Europe almost until the present day. About a hundred treatises are ascribed to him. He was great not only in his medical work, but in mathematics and astronomy, as well as philosophy. See *One White Race* by Joseph Sheban, page 241.

returned to this earth to register what it saw and heard in words of beauty.

If we examine the merit of Farid's work, we find him a holy man in the temple of free thought, a prince in the great kingdom of the imagination and a general in the mighty army of mysticism. That mighty army inches steadily, nevertheless, toward the kingdom of God, conquering on its way the petty and mean things in life, ever seeking the magnificent and the majestic.

Al Farid lived in an era (1119-1220) void of creativity and original thinking. He lived among a people who parroted tradition, energetically commenting upon and explaining the great heritage of Islamic learning and philosophy.

He was a genius; a genius is a miracle. Al Farid deserted his times and shunned his milieu, seeking seclusion to write and to unite in his universal poetry the unknown with the known in life.

Al Farid did not choose his theme from daily events as Al Mutanabbi[2] had done. He did not busy himself with the enigma of life as Maary[2] had done. Rather, he shut his eyes against the world in order to see beyond it, and he closed his ears against the tumult of the earth so that he could hear the eternal songs.

This, then, was Al Farid, a soul pure as the rays of the sun, a heart aflame, a mind as serene as a mountain lake, his poetry reaching beyond the dreams of those who came before and after him.

2. Both Mutanabbi and Maary are great Arab poets.

There exists between Al Ghazali and St. Augustine
a spiritual unity. They represent two eras, but one idea
despite the difference in the time, the religion and the
society of their days. That idea is that there is a desire
deep within the soul which drives man from the seen
to the unseen, to philosophy and to the divine.

Al Ghazali gave up a life of ease and a high position
to follow a life of asceticism and mysticism.[3] He searched
for those thin lines which join the end of science to
the beginning of religion. He searched for that hidden
chalice in which the intelligence and experience of man
is blended with his aspirations and his dreams.

St. Augustine had searched for the same chalice
more than five centuries earlier. Whoever reads *The
Confessions* of St. Augustine finds that he used the
world and its fruit as a ladder to climb to consciousness of eternal truth.

However, I have found Al Ghazali nearer the secret
and the heart of the matter than St. Augustine. This
could be attributed to the difference in their eras; also,
to Al Ghazali's inheritance of the teaching and philosophies of the Arabs and Greeks who preceded him, as
well as St. Augustine's bequest. By this I mean the

3. Al Ghazali was a professor at the college in Bagdad. He
gave up his chair suddenly, left his family and devoted himself
to the ascetic life. He left 69 works, one of them in thirteen
volumes. Al Ghazali wandered through Damascus, Jerusalem,
Hebron, Mecca, Medina and Alexandria, but returned to Tas,
Arabia, where he died.

matters that one mind hands down to another just as customs and dress represent certain eras.

I found in Ghazali a golden chain linking those mystics of India who preceded him with the deists who followed him. There is something of Al Ghazali in Buddhism and there is some of Ghazali's thinking in Spinoza and Blake.

Al Ghazali is highly respected among learned Orientalists of the West. The religious among them consider his the greatest and noblest concepts born of Islam. Strange as it seems, I saw on the wall of the fifteenth-century church in Venice a mural including Al Ghazali among the philosophers, saints and theologians whom, in the Middle Ages, the Church considered the corner-stones and pillars of its spiritual temple.

* *

Gibran, in his articles about Avicenna, Al Farid and Al Ghazali, left no doubt about his admiration for these great Arabic philosophers and made clear his belief in the philosophy of Avicenna: "There is no poem . . . nearer my own beliefs and my spiritual inclination than that poem of Avicenna."

Gibran followed the definition of Averröes: "Space and matter are in God." Gibran said: "We are the breath and the fragrance of God." Gibran believed in the existence of God, in the existence of the soul and its rebirth, but not according to the doctrine of Nirvana.

Those who follow the doctrine of Nirvana believe that after death the soul enters the bodies of lower animals or the bodies of other human beings; and that it passes from one body to another until it is purified. It then returns to the dwelling place of its god.

Gibran did not accept the purification process. He believed that the soul comes back to finish what the man abandoned when he left the earth.

In an article about reincarnation and Nirvana, "The poet from Baalbek," written in Arabic, Gibran stated that the soul returns to an equal status. He wrote: "And the prince inquired, saying, 'Tell us, O sage, will the gods ever restore me to this world as a prince and bring back the deceased poet to life? Will my soul become incarnated in a body of a great king's son and the soul of the poet in the body of a great poet? Will the sacred laws permit him to face eternity composing poetry about life? Will I be able to shower him with gifts?' And the sage answered the prince saying: 'Whatever the soul longs for it will attain. The sacred laws which restore the Spring after the passing of the winter will reinstate you a prince and will reinstate the poet as a poet.' "

Gibran wrote in *The Prophet*:
Fare you well, people of Orphalese
This day has ended.

Forget not that I shall come back to you.
A little while, and my longing shall
    gather dust and foam for another body.
A little while, a moment of rest upon
    the wind, and another woman shall
    bear me.

51

Gibran wrote in the last page of *The Garden of the Prophet*:

O, Mist, my sister, my sister, Mist,
I am one with you now.
No longer am I a self.
The walls have fallen,
And the chains have broken;
I rise to you, a mist,
And together we shall float upon the sea until
life's second day,
When dawn shall lay you, dewdrops in
a garden,
And me a babe upon the breast of a woman.

In the late eighteenth-century materialism gained wide hold in Europe. The economic life of society became more important than religious ethics. The theory of natural selection was held to justify might against right, whether between individuals or nations.

Nietzsche and many other writers made the "self" the center of something approaching worship. Nietzsche even proclaimed that God was dead.

John A. T. Robinson maintained that Nietzsche was not an atheist, that he was trying to free man from the God who is a tyrant, who impoverishes, enslaves and annihilates man. He was trying to get rid of the kindly old man who could be pushed into one corner while men "got on with business."

One of Gibran's biographers has claimed that Gibran became acquainted with the work of Nietzsche and was even influenced by it.

Gibran demanded that his people in the Middle East should revolt against Turkish rule. But at no time did he ever deny the existence of God.

We know that Gibran believed in God and in the immortality of the soul. But did he believe that man and his soul required guidance and, if so, what kind of guidance?

It is essential that we know the traditions and auspices of Gibran's background to answer the questions raised by his works. Gibran was born to the daughter of a Maronite priest, was baptized by his grandfather in rites employing Syriac, or Aramaic, the language Christ spoke. The Maronite Church is typical of Lebanon's tradition of being not only physically but philosophically and intellectually at the crossroads of the world. The Maronite rite came to Lebanon directly from the Church of Antioch, but it is Roman Catholic, preserving its ancient language and rituals through the Patriarch of Antioch and the Middle East, but preserving also its allegiance to Rome. Maronite priests are often married, for a married man may become a priest. A man may not, however, marry after he takes the Maronite vows of the priesthood.

At the age of five, Gibran was sent to a village school under the auspices of the Maronite Church. When he was eleven, he had memorized all the Psalms. At thirteen, he entered Al Hikmat, a church college, where he remained for five years. At Al Hikmat, he studied with Father Joseph Haddad, whom Gibran described as "the only man who ever taught me anything."

In his maturity, after he had written *The Prophet,*

53

Gibran wrote *Jesus, the Son of Man,* a book whicn reflects Gibran's deep knowledge of the Bible and of both Western and Eastern thought; for Gibran wrote not only of Arab philosophers but also of such men as St. Augustine, whom the West considers the Father of Latin theology. Augustine, nevertheless, was of Lebanese origin (Punic or Phoenician); he had been educated in the Phoenician schools of Carthage and was 33 before he accepted Christianity. Augustine accepted St. Paul's belief in man's original sin, but defined evil as that evil that man does voluntarily; St. Augustine wrote that only with help and through grace could man attain salvation, a premise which is now an orthodox doctrine of the Church.

Also, even a cursory review of Gibran's works reveals that he had familiarized himself with the works of the ancient Lebanese, the high priests of Eshtar, Baal and Tamuz; he knew, too, Moses, the Prophets, the Beatitudes, and had read deeply of both Christian and Islamic theology. Gibran's thirst had taken him to the fountains of Buddha, Zoroaster, Confucius, Voltaire, Rousseau, Nietzsche, Jefferson, Emerson and even to Lincoln. Gibran recognized that our religions advocate discipline and guidance, first through ceremonial practices, and secondly through prescribed ethical conduct.

Although religious rites vary greatly, Western ethics today are still those codified by Gibran's ancestors along the eastern shore of the Mediterranean, rules which advocate prudence, temperance, courage, justice, love, mercy and self-sacrifice.

Gibran was a rebel, but only against ceremonial practice, not against the ethos of his ancestors. Barbara Young, Gibran's secretary in the latter years of his life, has written, "Organized religion had no attraction for this man." But careful reading proves that Gibran was not agnostic; his anger was against religion as it was practiced, not against the religious man.

When Gibran was growing to manhood, the Turks ruled Lebanon, and the Maronite Church accepted a feudal role in order to survive within an Islamic society. Buttressing the feudal position of the church, the Christian Lebanese, the Maronites, zealously donated more lands to the church than it could cultivate; therefore, as the church turned more and more to the practice of sharecropping, it became increasingly a feudal master and employer of its own members. As the Church's secular power grew, some of its hierarchy, its bishops and priests, used their position and the Church's power to advance and enrich friends and relatives.

Gibran grew up too near the Church not to recognize its worldliness. He lost his first love to the nephew of a rapacious bishop. Then, leaving his own land, he saw the contrast provided by liberty, tolerance and freedom in America. His rebellion against the religious, then, was not only personal, but grew from the very ethos he had first learned from the religious.

Gibran later wrote a story in Arabic called "Kahlil the Heretic," in which a novice tries to convince the monks to distribute all their possessions and to go preach among the poor. "Let us restore to the needy the vast lands of the convent and let us give back the riches we have taken from them. Let us disperse and

55

teach the people to smile because of the bounty of heaven and to rejoice in the glories of life and of freedom.

"The hardships we shall encounter among the people shall be more sanctifying and more exalting than the ease and serenity we accept in this place. The sympathy that touches a neighbor's heart is greater than virtue practiced unseen in this convent. A word of compassion for the weak, the criminal and the sinner is more magnificent than long, empty prayers droned in the temple."

The monks, of course, unable to make Kahlil obey their rules, throw him out of the monastery.

"The feudal lord proclaims from his castle that the Sultan has appointed him as overlord to the people and the priest proclaims from his altar that God has appointed him as guardian of their souls.

"The feudal lord binds the poor 'fellah's' arms while the priest filches from his pockets. Between the lord representing the law and the priest representing God, the bodies and the souls of the people of Lebanon wither and die."

In another story, also written in Arabic, "John the Madman," Gibran tells of John's reading the New Testament, which ordinary men were forbidden to read.

One day, reading and meditating, John neglected his herd, the heifers slowly wandering into the monastery's pasture. The monks kept the heifers and demanded payment for damages. Unable to pay, John's mother ransomed the herd by giving the monks her heirloom necklace in payment. Thus John became a crusader against the church, a preacher in the public square:

"Come again, O Jesus, to drive the vendors of thy faith from thy sacred temple. . . . They fill the skies with smoke from their candles and incense but leave the faithful hungry."

The monks had John arrested and refused to free him until his father testified that he was insane. Therefore no one listened to John because the public was led to believe he was a madman.

Gibran, writing a friend about "John the Madman," said, "I found that earlier writers, in attacking the tyranny of some of the clergy, attacked the practice of religion. They were wrong because religion is a belief natural to man. But using religion as an excuse for tyranny is wrong. That is why I made sure that John in my story was a powerful believer in Jesus, in his Gospel and in his teaching."

The ethics of the West are, of course, the products of religion. It is true that much of the Western world has separated the state from religion;[4] but our laws recognize Mosaic law in the prohibition against murder, theft and adultery and in recognition of each individual's property rights. Gibran, recognizing the traditions and ethos of religion, also urged prudence, temperance, courage, justice, love, mercy and self-negation. Nowhere, however, does he answer the question, "Is it possible to believe in God, to practice the ethics of reli-

4. See *One White Race,* by Joseph Sheban.

gion and to admit salvation without the rites of religion?" He does, however, recognize the question in his short poem in Arabic, "O Soul":

O Soul

by Gibran

O Soul, if I did not covet immortality, I would never have learned the song which has been sung through all of time.

Rather, I would have been a suicide, nothing remaining of me except my ashes hidden within the tomb.

O soul! if I had not been baptized with tears and my eyes had not been mascaraed by the ghosts of sickness, I would have seen life as through a veil, darkly.

O soul! life is a darkness which ends as in the sunburst of day.

The yearning of my heart tells me there is peace in the grave.

O soul! if some fool tells you the soul perishes like the body and that which dies never returns, tell him the flower perishes but the seed remains and lies before us as the secret of life everlasting.

8. "ASK NOT WHAT YOUR COUNTRY
CAN DO FOR YOU"

The feudal system disappeared in both the political and religious life of Lebanon. It is now an independent state with its president and parliament elected by the people. Some of the stories and articles written by Gibran fifty years ago are a matter of history, but others are as modern as today's political situation, remaining timeless.

On the walls of many American homes hangs a plaque commemorating the statement of the late President John F. Kennedy:

Ask not what your country can do for you,
but ask what you can do for your country.

This statement appeared in an article written by Gibran in Arabic, over fifty years ago. The heading of that article can be translated either "The New Deal" or "The New Frontier."

The article was directed to Gibran's people in the Middle East, but its philosophy and its lesson will continue as long as man lives in a free society. Hence we offer the translation of the whole article:

"The New Frontier"

by Gibran

There are in the Middle East today[1] two challenging ideas: old and new.

The old ideas will vanish because they are weak and exhausted.

There is in the Middle East an awakening that defies slumber. This awakening will conquer because the sun is its leader and the dawn is its army.

In the fields of the Middle East, which have been a large burial ground, stand the youth of Spring calling the occupants of the sepulchers to rise and march toward the new frontiers.

When the Spring sings its hymn the dead of the winter rise, shed their shrouds and march forward.

There is on the horizon of the Middle East a new awakening; it is growing and expanding; it is reaching and engulfing all sensitive, intelligent souls; it is penetrating and gaining the sympathy of noble hearts.

The Middle East, today, has two masters. One is deciding, ordering, being obeyed; but he is at the point of death.

But the other one is silent in his conformity to law and order, calmly awaiting justice; he is a powerful giant who knows his own strength, confident in his existence and a believer in his destiny.

There are today, in the Middle East, two men: one of the past and one of the future. Which one are you?

1. Fifty years before this translation.

Come close; let me look at you and let me be assured by your appearance and conduct if you are one of those coming into the light or going into the darkness.

Come and tell me who and what are you.

Are you a politician asking *what your country can do for you* or a zealous one asking *what you can do for your country.*

If you are the first, then you are a parasite; if the second, then you are an oasis in a desert.

Are you a merchant utilizing the need of society for the necessities of life, for monopoly and exorbitant profit? Or a sincere, hard-working and diligent man facilitating the exchange between the weaver and the farmer? Are you charging a reasonable profit as a middleman between supply and demand?

If you are the first, then you are a criminal whether you live in a palace or a prison. If you are the second, then you are a charitable man whether you are thanked or denounced by the people.

Are you a religious leader, weaving for your body a gown out of the ignorance of the people, fashioning a crown out of the simplicity of their hearts and pretending to hate the devil merely to live upon his income?

Or are you a devout and a pious man who sees in the piety of the individual the foundation for a progressive nation, and who can see through a profound search in the depth of his own soul a ladder to the eternal soul that directs the world?

If you are the first, then you are a heretic, a disbeliever in God even if you fast at day and pray by night.

If you are the second, then you are a violet in the garden of truth even though its fragrance is lost upon the nostrils of humanity or whether its aroma rises into that rare air where the fragrance of flowers is preserved.

Are you a newspaperman who sells his idea and his principle in the slave market, who lives on the misery of people like a buzzard which descends only upon a decaying carcass?

Or are you a teacher on the platform of the city gathering experience from life and presenting it to the people as sermons you have learned?

If you are the first, then you are a sore and an ulcer. If you are the second, then you are a balsam and a medicine.

Are you a governor who denigrates himself before those who appoint him and denigrates those whom he is to govern, who never raises a hand unless it is to reach into pockets and who does not take a step unless it is for greed?

Or are you the faithful servant who serves only the welfare of the people?

If you are the first, then you are as a tare in the threshing floor of the nation; and if the second, then you are a blessing upon its granaries.

Are you a husband who allows for himself what he disallows for his wife, living in abandonment with the key of her prison in his boots, gorging himself with his favorite food while she sits, by herself, before an empty dish?

Or are you a companion, taking no action except

hand in hand, nor doing anything unless she gives her thoughts and opinions, and sharing with her your happiness and success?

If you are the first, then you are a remnant of a tribe which, still dressing in the skins of animals, vanished long before leaving the caves; and if you are the second, then you are a leader in a nation moving in the dawn toward the light of justice and wisdom.

Are you a searching writer full of self-admiration, keeping his head in the valley of a dusty past, where the ages discarded the remnant of its clothes and useless ideas?

Or are you a clear thinker examining what is good and useful for society and spending your life in building what is useful and destroying what is harmful?

If you are the first, then you are feeble and stupid, and if you are the second, then you are bread for the hungry and water for the thirsty.

Are you a poet, who plays the tambourine at the doors of emirs, or the one who throws the flowers during weddings and who walks in processions with a sponge full of warm water in his mouth, a sponge to be pressed by his tongue and lips as soon as he reaches the cemetery?

Or have you a gift which God has placed in your hands on which to play heavenly melodies which draw our hearts toward the beautiful in life?

If you are the first, then you are a juggler who evokes in our soul that which is contrary to what you intend.

If you are the second, then you are love in our hearts and a vision in our minds.

In the Middle East there are two processions: One procession is of old people walking with bent backs, supported with bent canes; they are out of breath though their path is downhill.

The other is a procession of young men, running as if on winged feet, and jubilant as with musical strings in their throats, surmounting obstacles as if there were magnets drawing them up the mountainside and magic enchanting their hearts.

Which are you and in which procession do you move?

Ask yourself and meditate in the still of the night; find if you are a slave of yesterday or free for the morrow.

I tell you that the children of yesteryears are walking in the funeral of the era that they created for themselves. They are pulling a rotted rope that might break soon and cause them to drop into a forgotten abyss. I say that they are living in homes with weak foundations; as the storm blows — and it is about to blow — their homes will fall upon their heads and thus become their tombs. I say that all their thoughts, their sayings, their quarrels, their compositions, their books and all their work are nothing but chains dragging them because they are too weak to pull the load.

But the children of tomorrow are the ones called by life, and they follow it with steady steps and heads high, they are the dawn of new frontiers, no smoke will veil their eyes and no jingle of chains will drown out their voices. They are few in number, but the difference is as between a grain of wheat and a stack of hay. No one knows them but they know each other.

They are like the summits, which can see and hear each other — not like caves, which cannot hear or see. They are the seed dropped by the hand of God in the field, breaking through its pod and waving its sapling leaves before the face of the sun. It shall grow into a mighty tree, its root in the heart of the earth and its branches high in the sky.

9. SOLITUDE AND SECLUSION

by Gibran

Life is an island in an ocean of solitude and seclusion.

Life is an island, rocks are its desires, trees its dreams, and flowers its loneliness, and it is in the middle of an ocean of solitude and seclusion.

Your life, my friend, is an island separated from all other islands and continents. Regardless of how many boats you send to other shores or how many ships arrive upon your shores, you yourself are an island separated by its own pains, secluded in its happiness and far away in its compassion and hidden in its secrets and mysteries.

I saw you, my friend, sitting upon a mound of gold, happy in your wealth and great in your riches and believing that a handful of gold is the secret chain that links the thoughts of the people with your own thoughts and links their feeling with your own.

I saw you as a great conqueror leading a conquering army toward the fortress, then destroying and capturing it.

On second glance I found beyond the wall of your treasures a heart trembling in its solitude and seclusion like the trembling of a thirsty man within a cage of gold and jewels, but without water.

I saw you, my friend, sitting on a throne of glory,

surrounded by people extolling your charity, enumerating your gifts, gazing upon you as if they were in the presence of a prophet lifting their souls up into the planets and stars. I saw you looking at them, contentment and strength upon your face, as if you were to them as the soul is to the body.

On the second look I saw your secluded self standing beside your throne, suffering in its seclusion and quaking in its loneliness. I saw that self stretching its hands as if begging from unseen ghosts. I saw it looking above the shoulders of the people to a far horizon, empty of everything except its solitude and seclusion.

I saw you, my friend, passionately in love with a beautiful woman, filling her palms with your kisses as she looked at you with sympathy and affection in her eyes and the sweetness of motherhood on her lips; I said, secretly, that love has erased his solitude and removed his seclusion and he is now within the eternal soul which draws toward itself, with love, those who were separated by solitude and seclusion.

On the second look I saw behind your soul another lonely soul, like a fog, trying in vain to become a drop of tears in the palm of that woman.

Your life, my friend, is a residence far away from any other residence and neighbors.

Your inner soul is a home far away from other homes named after you. If this residence is dark, you cannot light it with your neighbor's lamp; if it is empty you cannot fill it with the riches of your neighbor; were it in the middle of a desert, you could not move it to a garden planted by someone else.

Your inner soul, my friend, is surrounded with solitude and seclusion. Were it not for this solitude and this seclusion you would not be you and I would not be I. If it were not for that solitude and seclusion, I would, if I heard your voice, think myself to be speaking; yet, if I saw your face, I would imagine that I were looking into a mirror.

10. THE SEA

by Gibran

In the still of the night
As man slumbers behind the folds,
the forest proclaims:
  "I am the power
  Brought by the sun from
  the heart of the earth."
The sea remains quiet, saying to itself,
  "I am the power."

The rock says,
  "The ages erected me as a monument
  Until the Judgment Day";
The sea remains silent saying to itself,
  "I am the monument."

The wind howls
  "I am strong,
  I separate the heavens from the earth."
The sea remains quiet, saying to itself,
  "The wind is mine."

The river says
  "I am the pure water
  That quenches the thirst of the earth";

The sea remains silent saying to itself,
"The river is mine."

The summit says,
"I stand high like a star
In the center of the sky."
The sea remains quiet saying to itself,
"The summit is mine."

The brain says,
"I am a ruler;
The world is in those who rule";
The sea remains slumbering saying, in its sleep,
"All is mine."

11. HANDFUL OF BEACH SAND

by Gibran

When you tell your trouble to your neighbor you present him with a part of your heart. If he possesses a great soul, he thanks you; if he possesses a small one, he belittles you.

Progress is not merely improving the past; it is moving forward toward the future.

A hungry savage picks fruit from a tree and eats it; a hungry, civilized man buys it from a man who, in turn, buys it from the man who picks it.

Art is one step from the visibly known toward the unknown.

The earth breathes, we live; it pauses in breath, we die.

Man's eye is a magnifier; it shows him the earth much larger than it is.

I abstain from the people who consider insolence, bravery and tenderness cowardice. And I abstain from those who consider chatter wisdom and silence ignorance.

They tell me: If you see a slave sleeping, do not wake him lest he be dreaming of freedom.

I tell them: If you see a slave sleeping, wake him and explain to him freedom.

Contradiction is a lower degree of intelligence.

Bravery is a volcano; the seed of wavering does not grow on its crater.

The river continues on its way to the sea, broken the wheel of the mill or not.

The greater your joy or your sorrow, the smaller the world in your eyes.

Learning nourishes the seed but it gives you no seed of its own.

I use hate as a weapon to defend myself; had I been strong, I would never have needed that kind of weapon.

There are among the people murderers who have never committed murder, thieves who have never stolen and liars who have spoken nothing but the truth.

Keep me away from the wisdom which does not cry, the philosophy which does not laugh and the greatness which does not bow before children.

O great intelligent Being! hidden and existing in and for the universe, You can hear me because You are within me and You can see me because You are all-seeing; please drop within my soul a seed of Your wisdom to grow a sapling in Your forest and to give of Your fruit. Amen!

12. THE SAYINGS OF THE BROOK

by Gibran

I walked in the valley as the rising dawn spoke the
    secret of eternity,
And there a brook, on its course, was singing, calling
    and saying:
Life is not only a merriment;
Life is desire and determination.
Wisdom is not in words;
Wisdom is meaning within words.
Greatness is not in exalted position;
Greatness is for he who refuses position.

A man is not noble through ancestry;
How many noblemen are descendants of murderers?

Not everyone in chains is subdued;
At times, a chain is greater than a necklace.

Paradise is not in repentance;
Paradise is in the pure heart.

Hell is not in torture;
Hell is in an empty heart.

Riches are not in money alone;
How many wanderers were the richest of all men?

Not all the poor are scorned;
The wealth of the world is in a loaf of bread and a cloak.

Beauty is not in the face;
Beauty is a light in the heart.

Perfection is not for the pure of soul;
There may be virtue in sin.

This is what the brook said to the tree upon its banks;
Perhaps what the brook sang was of some of the secrets of the sea.

13. FOR HEAVEN'S SAKE, MY HEART!

by Gibran

For heaven's sake, my heart, keep secret your love,
    and hide the secret from those you see
    and you will have better fortune.
He who reveals secrets is considered a fool;
    silence and secrecy are much better for him
    who falls in love.
For heaven's sake, my heart, if someone asks,
"What has happened?," do not answer.
If you are asked, "Who is she?,"
Say she is in love with another
And pretend that it is of no consequence.
For heaven's sake, my love, conceal your passion;
    your sickness is also your medicine because love
    to the soul is as wine in a glass — what you
    see is liquid, what is hidden is its spirit.
For heaven's sake, my heart, conceal your troubles;
    then, should the seas roar and the skies fall,
    you will be safe.

14. THE ROBIN

by Gibran

O Robin, sing! for the secret of eternity
   is in song.

I wish I were as you, free from prisons and
   chains.

I wish I were as you; a soul flying over
   the valleys,
Sipping the light as wine is sipped from
   ethereal cups.

I wish I were as you, innocent, contented
   and happy
Ignoring the future and forgetting the past.

I wish I were as you in beauty, grace and
   elegance
With the wind spreading my wings for
   adornment by the dew.

I wish I were as you, a thought floating
   above the land
Pouring out my songs between the forest
   and the sky.

O Robin, sing! and disperse my anxiety.
I listen to the voice within your voice
   that whispers in my inner ear.

15. THE GREAT SEA

by Gibran

Yesterday, the far and the near yesterday,
   my soul and I walked to the Great Sea to wash
from ourselves, in its waters, the dust and dirt
of the earth. Arriving at the shore, we searched
for a secluded place far from the sight of others.

As we walked, we saw a man sitting upon a gray rock,
   in his hand a bag of salt from which he took one
handful at a time and threw it into the sea.
   My soul said, "This man believes in bad omens;
   He sees nothing of life except its shadows.
   No believer in bad omens should see our naked
      bodies.
   Let us leave; we can do no bathing here."

We left that spot and moved on to a bay.
There we saw a man standing on a white rock,
   and in his hand was a vase ornamented with precious
   stones.
From the vase he was taking cubes of sugar
   and throwing them into the sea.
      My soul said, "This man believes in good omens,
      and he expects to happen things which never
      happen.

Beware, for neither should we let him
see our naked selves."

We walked on until we came to a man
standing by the shore,
picking up dead fish and throwing them
back into the sea.
My soul said, "This man is compassionate,
trying to bring back life to those
already dead. Let us keep away from him."

We continued on until we saw a man
tracing his own shadow on the sand.
The waves rolled across his sketches and erased them,
but he continued to retrace his work.
My soul said, "He is a mystic, creating
images to worship in his own imagination.
Let us leave him alone also."

We walked on again until we saw a man
in a quiet bay skimming the foam off the waves
and putting them into an agate jar.
My soul said, "He is a visionary like
one who tries to weave a garment from
spider threads. He is not worthy of
seeing our naked bodies."

We moved ahead until suddenly we heard
a voice calling, "This is the sea!
This is the frightful sea!" We looked for
the source of the voice, and we found a
man with his back turned to the sea. In his

hand he held a shell over his ear, listening
to its murmur.
  My soul said, "He is a materialist,
    who closes his eyes to those things
    in the universe which he cannot understand
    and occupies himself with trifles."

My soul was saddened, and in a bitter voice said:
  "Let us leave these shores. There is no
    secluded place here for us to bathe.
    I will not comb my hair in this wind,
    nor will I open my bosom in this open space,
    nor will I undress and stand naked in this
    bright light."

My soul and I then left this great sea in search
  of a greater sea.

16. SEVEN REPRIMANDS

by Gibran

I reprimanded my soul seven times!

The first time: when I attempted to exalt
myself by exploiting the weak.

The second time: when I feigned a limp
before those who were crippled.

The third time: when, given a choice,
I elected the easy rather than the difficult.

The fourth time: when I made a mistake
I consoled myself with the mistakes of others.

The fifth time: when I was docile because of fear
and then claimed to be strong in patience.

The sixth time: when I held my garments upraised
to avoid the mud of Life.

The seventh time: when I stood in hymnal to God
and considered the singing a virtue.

17. DURING A YEAR NOT REGISTERED IN HISTORY

by Gibran

. . . In that moment appeared from behind
the willow trees a beautiful girl with hair
that touched the ground. She stood beside
the sleeping youth and touched his tender
brow with her silken soft hand.

He looked at her through sleepy eyes as
though awakened by the rays of the sun.

When he realized the Emir's daughter was
standing beside him he fell upon his knees as
Moses had done when he saw the burning bush.

He attempted to speak. Words failed him
but his tearful eyes supplanted his tongue.

The young girl embraced him, kissed his
lips; then she kissed his eyes, drying his copious
tears and lips with her kisses.

In a voice softer than the tone of the reed,
she said: "I saw you, sweetheart, in my dreams;
I looked upon your face in my loneliness. You
are the lost consort of my soul and the other
better half from which I was separated when I was
ordered to come into this world."

"I came here secretly to join you,

sweetheart. Do not fear; you are now in
my arms. I left the glory which surrounds
my father and came to follow you to the end
of the world, and to drink with you the cup
of life and death."

"Come, sweetheart, let us go into the
wilderness, away from civilization."

And the lovers walked into the forest,
into the darkness of the night, fearing
neither an Emir nor the phantoms of the
darkness.

18. THE WOMEN IN THE LIFE
OF GIBRAN

Gibran's Mother, Kamila

Gibran recognized the influence of women in his life. He once wrote: "I am indebted for all that I call 'I' to women ever since I was an infant. Women opened the windows of my eyes and the doors of my spirit. Had it not been for the woman-mother, the woman-sister and the woman-friend, I would have been sleeping among those who disturb the serenity of the world with their snores."

There were many women in Gibran's life, his biographers agree.

Gibran's mother was especially important in his life because of circumstances which directed her own life. After she married, she and her husband migrated to Brazil, where he took sick and died, leaving her with her infant son, Peter. The mother returned with her son to the home of her father, Stephen Rahmy, a Maronite priest.

The man who was to become Gibran's father, heard her singing one day in her father's garden, fell in love with her and soon they were married.

Kahlil Gibran was born December 6, 1883, followed by two sisters, Mariana and Sultana. Their mother taught them music, Arabic and French. As they grew older a tutor was brought into the home to teach them English.

Later they were sent to city schools. They were often taken to church, where their grandfather, a capable priest, served Mass and preached.

In the Maronite church, in certain ceremonies, the whole congregation participates, chanting in Syriac, the language Christ spoke. The effect of the Maronite ceremonies remained with Gibran the rest of his life, a letter he wrote in later years acknowledged his debt to the church.

The religious bent of Gibran's mother, her beautiful voice in church and the religious atmosphere of the family molded Gibran's character. This effect is apparent in Gibran's book, *Jesus, the Son of Man*.

As Gibran reached the age of twelve, his half-brother, Peter, reached the age of eighteen.

Peter was thus ready to go out on his own and, like all the Lebanese (Phoenicians) who have used the seas as their highways for thousands of years, set his heart on America.

Gibran's mother, unwilling to have her children separate, brought Peter, Kahlil and the two girls to Boston. Kahlil's father protested, for he owned large properties, collected taxes for the government, and in season did business as a cattle dealer. However, the fables from America — that the streets were paved with gold and the prospect of immediate riches — overwhelmed Peter, and he decided to bring the family to America, Kahlil's blond, blue-eyed father remaining in Lebanon,

Some of Gibran's biographers did not know that a cattle dealer in the Middle East is actually a sheep dealer, because sheep are imported to Lebanon, from Syria, from Iraq and sometimes even from Turkey. Actually, transporting sheep from Turkey without benefit of trucks, with few rail facilities, with little feed and water, is harder and more speculative than cattle droving in the United States. Kahlil's biographers, in their confusion, wrote that his father was a shepherd.

In Boston, Peter opened a grocery store, the other children being sent to school. At the age of fourteen Kahlil decided to go back to Lebanon to complete his education in Arabic. His mother, realizing the talent and ambition of her son, consented to have him return to Beirut to enter the College of Al Kikmat.

Gibran remained in the college five years, spending the summers near the cedars and traveling with his father through the Middle East. After his five years were over, Gibran visited Greece, Italy and Spain on his way to Paris to study art (1901-1903).

Gibran was called back to the States because his younger sister, Sultana, had died and his mother was very sick. His mother remained bedridden nearly fifteen months before she died. During this time his half-brother Peter also died. It was the greatest shock in Gibran's life. The family was very close and its members had made great sacrifice to educate him. Mariana miraculously survived the tuberculosis which decimated Kahlil's family. Gibran's feelings toward his mother are more eloquently expressed by his own words from *The Broken Wings*:

"Mother is everything in this life; she is consolation in time of sorrowing and hope in time of grieving and power in moments of weakness. She is the fountainhead of compassion, forbearance and forgiveness. He who loses his mother loses a bosom upon which he can rest his head, the hand that blesses, and eyes which watch over him."

Micheline

One biographer has stated that Gibran met, in Boston, a beautiful and vivacious girl named Emilie Michel, nicknamed Micheline. He also stated that Micheline followed Gibran to Paris, that she asked him to marry her and when he refused she left Gibran's apartment and vanished forever. Some biographers accepted this story; others did not mention the girl by name. Offered as proof by some who mentioned Micheline were two items: first, that Gibran had painted her before he left for Paris; second, the dedication of one of his books to Micheline.

I made a special effort to determine the existence of this beautiful girl. I visited the Museum of Gibran in Lebanon, where I asked the curator to direct me to the painting Micheline. Pointing to one of the paintings on the wall he said, "This is what is considered to be the painting of Micheline."

This painting has no identifying marks whatsoever. It is not even signed by Gibran. But then only a few of his paintings are signed. I found no facts to show that this was the painting of Micheline; I found no correspondence between Gibran and Micheline.

The reprints of Gibran's Arabic books, as stated earlier, lack information as to the date of first publication. They also lack dedications. After a long search I obtained copies of the earlier editions which contain dedications; I found that Micheline was not mentioned.

The dedication I found read thus:

"To the soul that embraced my soul, to the heart that poured its secrets into my own heart, to the hand that kindled the flame of my emotions, I dedicate this book."

In Paris Gibran lived and worked with a close friend, Joseph Hoyek, who wrote a book about their two years together. The two young men did not live in the same apartment; however, they met daily and often shared the cost of a model for the sake of saving money. Hoyek wrote about the girls they met, the restaurants in which they ate. He named Olga, a Russian girl, another named Rosina, and an Italian girl who was the most beautiful model they hired, but Hoyek made no mention of Micheline.

Therefore, until further evidence is available, I withhold my decision that Micheline ever existed.

Mary Haskell or Mary Khoury?

In 1904 Gibran borrowed twenty dollars and arranged for an exhibition of his paintings. One of those who visited that exhibit was a Miss Mary E. Haskell, who became his friend. Later, she paid his way to

Paris to further his art studies. One biographer said that Gibran thereafter asked her to check each of his manuscripts before he submitted it to his publisher.

Gibran's novel *The Broken Wings* was dedicated to M. E. H. However, the administrator of Gibran's estate insists that the woman who helped Gibran financially was a wealthy woman named Mary Khoury. The executor of the estate was the personal physician of Mary Khoury, and had seen in her apartment several of Gibran's paintings and statues on which Gibran had written in Arabic: "Do not blame a person for drinking lest he is trying to forget something more serious than drinking." The doctor further reports that she, Mary Khoury, agreed to have her letters from Gibran published. He also claims those letters were given to a friend for editing, and that both the friend and Mary Khoury have since died. Thus the letters and paintings fell into unknown hands.

According to Mary Khoury, Gibran spent many evenings, in the later days of his life, at her apartment.

The existence of letters from Gibran to Mary Khoury was verified independently by a reliable Lebanese reporter who explained that he had read some of them and that Mary Khoury had promised to have these letters released after they were edited. When I asked the newsman if the letters were business or love letters, he emphasized that they were love letters.

Nevertheless, the mystery remains about the benefactress in Kahlil Gibran's life: Was she Mary Haskell or Mary Khoury — or both?

Barbara Young

Barbara Young knew Gibran the last seven years of his life, during which time she became the first of his disciples to shout his praise in a biography, *The Man From Lebanon*.

"If he, Gibran, had never written a poem or painted a picture, his signature upon the page of eternal record would still be inerasable. The power of his individual consciousness has penetrated the consciousness of the age, and the indwelling of his spirit is timeless and deathless. "This is Gibran," wrote Barbara Young.

In 1923 Barbara heard a reading from *The Prophet*. She wrote to Gibran expressing her admiration. She received "his gracious invitation to come to this studio 'to talk about poetry' and to see the pictures."

"So I went," she wrote, "to the old West Tenth Street building, climbed the four flights of stairs and found him there, smiling, welcoming me as though we were old friends indeed."

Barbara was taller than Gibran, of light complexion, beautifully built. Her family came from Bideford, in Devon, England. By profession, she was an English teacher, she operated a book store, and she lectured about Gibran the rest of her life after that first climb of the four flights of stairs. After Gibran's death, she assembled and put together the chapters of his unfinished book, *Garden of the Prophet*, and arranged for its publication.

Barbara Young and other biographers have described Gibran as being slender, of medium height, five feet-four inches, as having large, sleepy, brown eyes fringed by long lashes, chestnut hair, and a generous mustache framing full lips. His body was strong and he possessed a powerful grip. In some of his letters he mentioned that the beating of his heart was becoming normal again.

Barbara Young was with Gibran at the hospital when he passed away. Soon afterward she packed the precious paintings and effects left in the studio where Gibran had lived for eighteen years, and sent them to his home town of Bcherri in Lebanon.

During her speaking tours Barbara exhibited more than sixty paintings of Gibran's work. What became of this collection or any unfinished work, papers or letters she may have had depends on the generosity of those who bought, received or inherited these objects. Until they come forward, there will never be a complete biography of Gibran, particularly that part dealing with Barbara Young.

How close a relationship existed during these seven years can be answered, in part, by excerpts from Barbara's own writing.

Barbara never lived with Gibran. She kept her own apartment in the city of New York.

One Sunday, Barbara wrote, accepting an invitation from Gibran, she went to the studio. Gibran was writing a poem; he was at his desk when she arrived. While composing Gibran usually paced the floor and then he would sit down to write a line or two.

"I waited while he repeated his writing and his walking again and again. Then a thought came to me. The next time he walked I went and seated myself at his table and took up his pencil. When he turned he saw me sitting there.

" 'You make the poem and I'll write it,' I said."

After much protest Gibran consented to try it. He was pleased with the experiment.

" 'Well, you and I are two poets working together.' He paused. Then after a silence, 'We are friends,' he said. 'I want nothing from you, and you want nothing from me. We share life.' "

As they worked together and as she became more acquainted with his manner of thought and his work, she told him of her determination to write a book about him. Gibran was pleased and "it was from that time on that he talked often of his childhood, his mother and family, and some events in his life."

One day Gibran asked, "Suppose you were compelled to give up — to forget all the words you know except seven — what are the seven words that you would keep?"

"I named only five," Barbara wrote. "God, Life, Love, Beauty, Earth . . . and asked Gibran what other words would he select and he answered, 'The most important words to keep are: You and I . . . without these two there would need to be no others' then Gibran selected the seven words: You, I, Give, God, Love, Beauty, Earth."

"Gibran liked a frugal supper in the studio," Barbara wrote, "particularly during a period of his life when he was entertained and being feasted. This one evening Gibran said that 'in the East there is a custom of eating all from one huge vessel. Let us have our soup tonight in one bowl!' So we did and Gibran humorously drew an imaginary line through the soup and said, 'this is your half of the soup and this other is my half. See to it that we neither one trespass upon the soup of the other!' Then laughter and a thorough enjoyment, each of his own half of the soup."

In another chapter Barbara wrote: "One evening when we were doing the book 'Sea and Foam,' I piled cushions on the floor and sat upon them instead of occupying my usual chair. Then I had a strange feeling of a familiarity about the gesture, and I said: 'I feel as if I've sat like this besides you many times — but I really haven't,' and Gibran answered, 'We have done this a thousand years ago, and we shall do it a thousand years hence.'

"And during the writing of the book 'Jesus, the Son of Man' the drama of some incident, now and again, was so overwhelming that I felt, and said, 'It is so real. It seems as if I had been there.' And his answer came, almost like a cry, 'You were there! And so was I!'"

It is appropriate, here, to tell that two years after the death of Gibran, Barbara Young and this author met in the city of Cleveland. She asked: "How long would it take to learn the Arabic language?" I explained to her that for the purpose of translating any of Gibran's works it would take many years to learn the classical version of the language; just to speak Arabic would be a different matter. In any event Arabic is a difficult language.

At that time I was studying for my law degree. I was neither interested in teaching Arabic nor contemplating the writing of a book about Gibran. She also told me that whenever Gibran painted a hand it was hers.

The most famous hand Gibran painted is the one with an eye in its palm. This painting was meant to represent the Phoenician Goddess Tanit. In honor of this Goddess, there are two cities in Lebanon called Eyetanit meaning "Eye of Tanit."

This pose, the eye nestled in the palm of the hand, appeared in Carthage in North Africa, carried there by Gibran's ancestors (the Phoenicians). The Phoenicians left one of these carvings of the hand of Tanit in Alabama before the arrival of Columbus.

Did Gibran see one of these hands in Lebanon, was the similarity a coincidence, or were Gibran and Barbara there when the Temples of Tanit were being built in Lebanon and Carthage long before the birth of Christ?

Barbara Young wrote that once when some women came to visit Gibran, they asked why he did not get married. He replied: "Well . . . you see it is like this. If I had a wife, and if I were painting or making poems, I should simply forget her existence for days at a time. And you know well that no loving woman would put up with such a husband for very long."

One of the women, not satisfied with the smiling answer, prodded still deeper, "But have you never been in love?" Controlling himself with difficulty, he said, "I will tell you a thing you may not know. The most highly sexed beings upon the planet are the creators, the poets, sculptors, painters, musicians . . . and so it

94

has been from the beginning. And among them sex is a beautiful and exalted gift. Sex is always beautiful, and it is always shy."

Barbara Young wrote the following paragraph, which we quote, without comment, leaving it to the reader to determine her place in the life of Gibran:

"It is always wise to be wary of the woman who appears out of nowhere and claims a great man for her own when he is dead. But if there be those who never say, 'Lord, Lord,' but who maintain a silence, doing his works, may it not be that these are the hands that have indeed ministered unto him, these the hearts that have perceived the intricacies of his myriad being? And for myself, I do not doubt that through the turbulent years of this man's life the ageless and universal cry for woman-comfort went out from his great loneliness, and that in the goodness of God, the cry was answered. To conclude otherwise would be the essence of stupidity."

Mariana

Mariana, being a young sister of Gibran, was not consulted about her family's migration.

She was not asked whether her brother should be sent to Lebanon and Europe. However, when tragedy struck, and her mother, her sister and brother Peter, who was the breadwinner, died of tuberculosis within two years, Mariana found herself alone with her brother Kahlil, whose literary work was awakening the Arab world and upsetting the Ottoman Empire. Mariana realized that literary greatness and money do not often meet until, and if, late in life. Gibran's education was in Arabic; thus his articles and books were not bringing in sufficient cash to furnish the necessities of life.

Mariana refused to let her brother alter his plans or to take a job which would interfere with his literary and art career. She sewed and knit to keep a home for herself and for her brother. She encouraged him to paint until he had a collection ready for showing. Mariana did not have the money to pay for the display of his works, but Gibran managed to borrow twenty dollars from a Lebanese woman, who lived in Boston then, and is still living now, in Lebanon, and considers Gibran's note her greatest possession.

The investment in Gibran's education paid dividends, not only to the literary world but in money as well. The estimate of the royalties from Gibran's books is over a million and a half dollars. These royalties are sent to his home town, Bcherri. However, he left to his sister, Mariana (Mary), who still lives in Boston, sufficient money for her to retire with security for the rest of her life. She was on very good terms with Barbara Young, who dedicated the book *The Man From Lebanon* to her.

May Ziadeh

May Ziadeh was Gibran's love on paper only; he never saw her. May was a Lebanese girl, whose family had moved to Egypt. An only child, she was educated in the Middle East and later went to Europe to study, later she wrote articles in her father's magazine and in other French and Arabic publications. Her parents' home was a meeting place for most of the prominent literary men in Egypt. Gibran's articles, appearing at this time, in many papers and magazines, were often a topic of discussion.

May, admiring Gibran's articles, decided to write to him. Fearing that he might disregard her letters as simply those from another admirer, she wrote, in the beginning, an introduction of herself. She explained that she wrote articles and books, and that much of her work appeared under the nom de plume, Isis Cubia. Then she proceeded to tell him the great effect his writing was having upon the Egyptian community.

Gibran was prompt in his answer. He wrote admiring her courage and thanking her for working toward the liberation of women in the Middle East. He told her that he was mailing her, in a separate package, a copy of his new book, *The Broken Wings*. And he tried to explain how he came to give it that title:

"I inherited from my mother ninety percent of my character and my disposition. This does not mean that I inherited her beauty and her humility, or her big heart. I recall that she told me once, when I was twenty years old, that it would have been much better for me and the people had I become a monk in one of the monasteries.

"I said, 'It is true except that I took you as a mother before I came into this world.'

"She replied, 'If you had not come, you would have remained an angel.'

"I answered, 'I am still an angel.'

"She smiled and asked, 'But where are your wings?'"

"I placed her arms on my shoulders and then said, 'These are my wings.'"

"She responded, 'But they are broken.'"

Gibran added in his letter: "My mother, since passed beyond the blue horizon, but her words, 'the broken wings' remained with me and I used them for the title of the novel I am sending to you. I appreciate your personal opinion."

May sent her opinion, admiring the book, but sharply disagreeing with Gibran, because in the story he condoned a married woman meeting with her former lover.

"Regardless of how innocent it was," May wrote, "it is a betrayal of the husband, it is a betrayal of the name she carries and it is a betrayal of society."

In the meantime, the intelligentsia of Egypt were planning to honor a Lebanese poet and Gibran was to be one of the speakers. Unable to attend, mainly because he didn't have the money, Gibran sent an article "The Poet of Baalbek"[1] to be read at the affair. The toastmaster, knowing about the correspondence between Gibran and May, asked her to read the article.

Even though it was May's first attempt at public speaking, her reading earned an ovation. Thus, she had auctioned her heart to Gibran. They corresponded until his death. May's letters were not all of love, for she criticized his writing frequently and prodded him to write on certain subjects.

1. Baalbek was the hometown of the poet being honored.

Once May wrote:

"The new Turkish governor arrived in Lebanon, and as usual, he began removing people from their jobs. He is following in the footsteps of his predecessors. The Lebanese people are prostrating themselves before his feet. When are we going to have among us men of courage? When are the Lebanese going to shake off the dust of insult? Why don't you write on this subject? The people respect your ideas, Gibran. Remind them they are men and men should not humble themselves."

Writing on the subject Gibran said:

"Woe to the nation that receives her conquerors beating the drums. Woe to the nation that hates oppression in her sleep and accepts it in her awakening. Woe to the nation that raises her voice only behind a coffin and prides itself only in the cemetery. Woe to a nation that does not revolt until her neck is placed on the scaffold."

Gibran wrote and asked May to come to the United States. She refused because she was a woman and custom did not permit her; she asked him to come to Egypt. Part of Gibran's letter said: "What can I say about my economic condition?

"A year or two ago I had some peace and quiet. But now the quietness has turned into tumult and peace into struggle. The people are demanding my days and nights. I am overwhelmed by their demands. Every once in a while I leave this great city to elude the people and to escape from myself. The American public is mighty. It never wearies or gets tired, is never exhausted, never sleeps and never dreams. If it dislikes you it destroys you with neglect and if it likes you it destroys you with its affection and demand.

"The day may yet come when I can escape to the Middle East. If it were not for this cage, whose bars I have wrought with my own hands — I would have taken the first ship going East. What man would desert a building whose stones he had hewn and polished his entire life even though it had become a prison?"

In one of her letters May wrote:

"I do not know what I am doing but I know that I love you. I fear love. I expect too much of love, and I fear that I never will receive all my expectations. . . . How dare I write this to you. . . . ? However, I thank God I am writing it and not saying it. If you were present I would have vanished after such a statement and disappeared until you had forgotten what I said.

"I blame myself for taking even this much liberty. Nevertheless, right or wrong, my heart is with you and the best thing it can do is to hover over you and guard you with compassion."

May's heart needed to hover only for a short time because Gibran's health was failing. He wrote:

"You know, May, every time I think of departing, that is, in death, I enjoy my thoughts and am contented to leave."

Gibran departed in 1931 at the age of forty-seven after nearly nineteen years of his love affair, on paper, with May Ziadeh.

Gibran was eighteen "when love opened his eyes by its magic rays and Salma was the first woman" to do it.

Gibran wrote a novel in Arabic about his first love. No other author could have narrated the events better than Gibran. However, biographers and Gibran's neighbors insist that Gibran's first girl was called Hala Eldaher and that the events of the story took place in Bcherri instead of Beirut.

Gibran intended to buy the monastery of Mar Sarkis where Salma once met him. This monastery was actually carved in a cliff for a safe refuge. To enter it in the old days required either a rope or a ladder. Mariana, Gibran's sister, bought it. A footpath was built later for the convenience of visitors who now bow humbly before the resting place of Gibran, who had wished to retire there in life but reached his refuge only in death.

Among his last letters exists evidence of Gibran's desire "to go to the Middle East, to Lebanon, to Bcherri, to Mar Sarkis, that hermitage carved in the rock and overlooking the most astonishing sight the eye could ever see of the whole valley." Gibran was longing for the "new life in the heart of nature; among the golden fields of wheat, the green meadows, the flocks of sheep being led to pasture, the roaring falls and the rising mist reflecting in the rays of the sun."

Salma is presented to the reader in *The Broken Wings,* Gibran's own love story which has been on the best-seller list in Arabic for more than forty years.